PREFACE

I would like to thank my wife, Elvia, and my daughter, Cynthia, for the encouragement that they gave me in working on this story. I would also like to thank Marjorie Fix (nee. Redbourn) and Mary Chow and several children for the help they gave me with the grammar, composition, style and content.

I would especially like to thank my son, Roy James Jr., commonly called, "Jim", for his contribution to the story. Many of the incidents in the story actually happened to Jim and I on some of our "adventures". His encouragement to write them down was a real impetus to do so. Thanks also to Cynthia for her contributions of many pictures and to my grandsons Ethan and Jimmy for posing for some of the pictures

Appreciation goes to the many friends and relatives who kept on encouraging me to put this story into print. However, the most appreciation of all goes to the Lord

Roy Hubbard

God who has been my strength and wisdom in all of my endeavours.

I desire that this story teach as well as entertain. References to the fishing industry, nature and other facets of life are intended to direct the youngster into learning about the British Columbia coast and its many facets. Also it is my desire to create an interest into developing a meaningful relationship with God through Christ Jesus and to incite an interest in reading God's Word.

I trust that this story will be a blessing to all who read it and so I invite you to discover the adventures of Willy.

Roy Hubbeard

TABLE OF CONTENTS

3

CHAPTER ONE: OFF TO THE SALTCHUCK

Willy was excited; not just excited but really, really, really excited. William Paul MacNeil was nine years old and this was to be his first fishing trip with his dad. William was commonly known simply as "Willy". His dad, Arthur, a tall muscular man with dark brown hair like Willy, often jokingly called his only son, "Wild Will" because of all of the interesting adventures in which Willy managed to get involved.

Mr. MacNeil owned a commercial fishing boat on the west coast of Canada called a hand troller or simply a troller. He made his living by fishing during the summer months in the Pacific Ocean. A troller has a cabin toward the front of the boat. On each side of the boat is a long pole called an outrigger that reaches far above the cabin. When these poles are lowered outwards so that they stick out from each side of the boat not quite level with the water, fishing lines are fastened to them so that many lures can trail behind the boat to catch fish.

Arthur MacNeil kept his boat tied up at the fishing boat wharves in Eaglecrest, their hometown. The local people called them "Fishermen's Docks". Eaglecrest was a little town of about 800 people that was nestled at the base of the Coastal Mountains that follow the Pacific Ocean coastline from Alaska down through British Columbia, Canada. The town looked out on Murphy's Cove to the west with the mountain to the east. Jutting out into the Pacific Ocean at the north end of town was a long arm of land called, "Prospector Point". The only highway to Eaglecrest ran south towards Powell River and the coastal area called The Sunshine Coast. The town was named Eaglecrest after the many bald eagles that nested in the cliffs of the nearby mountains. Willy could look up at the mountains from their back yard and see bald eagles and sometimes golden eagles soaring high overhead.

Because of the long hours that Arthur had to put in at sea, trying to catch enough salmon to make a living,

5

by the time he got home he just wanted to stay there. Going fishing just seemed like more work to him and he needed to rest. That is why Willy had never been on a fishing trip with his dad before.

That did not mean that Willy did not want to go out on his dad's fishing boat. Willy had begged his dad over and over to take him fishing with him for over 2 years. "Please dad," he would ask over and over, "let me go on a fishing trip with you." His dad would just reply, "Willy, you're too young to go out on that big boat. When you are older and more responsible I will take you on a fishing trip, just the two of us. We will be sport fishing instead of catching fish for a living. It will be more fun that way." Willy would just sadly reply, "Sure, dad. Sure." He doubted that the fishing trip would ever happen.

Arthur MacNeil watched his son grow up over the long months and decided that, at nine years of age, his son was old enough to be responsible enough to take a trip with him on his big boat. The one condition that he

6

had set down in order for them to take this fishing trip was that the weather had to be good. Willy's dad was concerned that since Willy had never gone out with him on the fishing boat, he might panic or get sick if they ran into stormy weather. It is bad enough on the ocean in good weather as the boat is tossed up and down and back and forth on the swells. Willy had heard his dad and other fishermen describe these wide rolling waves on the ocean and from the sound of it, the swells could get quite high. In fact, they can get several metres high and some people, having just got on the boat, often get sea-sick from the motion of the big waves. Arthur would sometimes laugh at these people when they were on his boat. He would tease them, calling them "landlubbers". He told them that they would be okay once they got their sea legs and they usually did just fine.

This fishing trip would be different from most of the fishing trips that his dad had gone on because this would be sport fishing just for fun, not a commercial trip to catch fish for the cannery that processed fish and canned them in a big building far up the coast from Murphy's Cove. That meant that they would have to use sport fishing gear instead of commercial gear. In that way it would be different for Willy's dad from the way he usually fished. They hoped to catch some salmon to take home with them to use for themselves.

Willy was filled with excitement as he looked forward to his first big fishing trip on his dad's big boat. They would be fishing for a fish that the local people called, "springs". The spring salmon were at their peak and he was sure they would do well. Willy had heard chinook salmon called "spring salmon" all his life and had seen them as his father brought home a few that he had saved for them after he had unloaded the boat at the cannery. He was certain that they would catch their limit of "springs" when they went out on Saturday.

Willy could hardly sleep Friday night as he began to imagine how much fun he would have the next day.

8

He had told all of his school friends about the upcoming fishing trip. Finally the long waiting was over and he would soon be getting on his dad's boat in an attempt to catch some "big ones". Long into the night Willy thought about fishing and the big fish they might soon catch. Finally his eyes grew heavy and the daydreams ended as Willy drifted off to sleep.

Willy dreamed about fish. He had dreams about big fish and small boats. He would awaken briefly and then go back to sleep. Then he would dream about salmon that looked like flashing fire. He also dreamed about how he and his dad reeled in salmon after salmon until there were no more fish to catch. He dreamed that there were so many fish on board that the boat began to sink and he would be scared. Then the dreams ceased and Willy fell into a deep undisturbed sleep.

Early Saturday morning around 5 a.m. Willy bounced out of bed, yelling, "Yahoo", eager to get going, forgetting all about his strange dreams of the night

9

before. He quickly changed from his pyjamas into a freshly washed pair of black pants and a red, green and white striped T-shirt that his mom had set out the night before. Then he literally bounced from his bedroom to the kitchen with excitement as he jumped for joy excitedly. He wanted to get going right away so he could catch some fish.

Willy found that his dad had already gotten up in order to prepare for their fishing trip. Willy's mom, Judy, had also found her way to the kitchen, although she was still dressed in her pink housecoat. She did not want to miss the excitement of seeing her "men", as she called them, head out on their first fishing trip together. Judy MacNeil was a slim, short blond lady who always seemed to wear a big smile. She was preparing a good hearty breakfast of oatmeal, toast and hot chocolate. Willy had decided that since they had to eat breakfast, he wanted bacon and eggs but his dad had warned him that greasy foods might help cause seasickness and should not be

10

eaten before taking a trip in a boat, especially on the ocean. Others dispute this advice but Mr. MacNeil firmly held to this belief.

As Mrs. MacNeil prepared breakfast, Willy and his dad sat by the radio and waited for the marine weather forecast. When the ad for Forester's Car Lot concluded, the weather forecaster's voice began. "Seas around Haida Gwaii (former the Queen Charlotte Islands) have a two foot chop with brisk winds gusting to 40 knots. A small boat warning is in effect. Heavy thunderstorms and strong winds up to 75 knots are expected by noon and continuing on into the rest of the day. Not a pleasant day for water lovers. Farther south, the Prospector Point area has rippled seas with mild breezes. The storm from the northwest Pacific is expected to miss this area completely. Should be a fairly good day on the water, but watch for any unexpected changes in cloud patterns. Could signal a shower or two. The Georgia Straight and Straits of Juan de Fuca have calm seas and beautiful sunny weather forecasted with the odd cloud scuttling across the sky. A fine day for water lovers in those areas!" Then another ad came on the radio and Arthur MacNeil turned off the radio.

"Sounds good for us", Willy's dad declared as he and Willy stood up.

Just then, Willy's mom announced that breakfast was ready. He hurried to the table and his father followed him to his usual place at the table. Willy started to eat when his dad asked, "Willy, aren't you forgetting something?"

"Oh, yeah, grace," Willy said in obvious disgust. "I just want to eat and get going."

Mr. MacNeil thanked God for the food and asked Him to bless the food, the day and mom as she stayed at home. Then he asked the Lord to keep them all safe. As soon as Mr. MacNeil said, "Amen", they began to eat. Willy was so excited that he gobbled down his food and gulped his hot chocolate so fast that he could hardly taste any of it.

"Slow down, young fella. You looked like you inhaled it," Willy's mom said to him chuckling. "After all, you have all day."

"All night too, if we need to," added his dad. "We've got lights to run at night too."

Willy replied, "But we gotta get going as soon as we can. We got to find the fish! Come on, Dad," Willy complained impatiently, "We want to spend as much time as possible fishing!" Then Willy raced out the door with "fisherman's hat" in his hand.

Willy

Ready

To Go

Fishing

Standing in the doorway wearing his fishing hat and Mackinaw with his fishing gear in hand, Willy looked out across the bay, imagining how much fun he was going to have. Mr. MacNeil quickly followed his son and joined him around the back of the house at their storage shed. They took out the fishing gear and then locked up the shed. Going around to the front door they met Mrs. MacNeil coming out of the house with some food for their trip. They loaded their truck with food and the other supplies that they were certain that they would need while they were out in the saltchuck. Willy had heard the fishermen call the salty water of the Pacific, "the saltchuck" as long as he could remember so he knew what this word meant.

Judy MacNeil took Willy's dad to the side of their truck so Will could not hear. "Please be careful'" she warned him. "I have a very uneasy feeling about their trip!"

"I will'" Arthur replied. Then they walked back to the tailgate of their truck.

14

The weather was perfect for an outing. The sun was shining brightly. A few scattered fluffy white clouds dotted the sky. A warm gentle breeze rippled the water slightly just as the weatherman had stated. The sky reflected the light blue colour of the summer sky. It looked like a perfect day for fishing. Since the weather forecast had said that a storm that was approaching the north end of Haida Gwaii was not expected to come close to where they would be fishing they were not concerned. The area to which they were going was expecting excellent weather all during the weekend.

Willy was so excited that he almost did not notice his mom giving him a kiss good-bye and wishing them lots of fishing success. "Let's go, dad," Willy shouted as he climbed into their truck and fastened his seatbelt. Mr. MacNeil kissed his wife good-bye and then climbed into the driver's seat. With a quick honk of the horn and a wave, Mr. MacNeil backed the truck out of the driveway on to the street. Then they drove down to the docks with their sport fishing equipment and supplies.

Mr. MacNeil had already charted their course and had given a copy of the chart to his wife. Mr. MacNeil knew that whenever anyone goes on a trip or outing it is important that at least one person knows where you have gone in case trouble arises or you get lost. When he got out of the truck Mr. MacNeil looked at the chart again to be certain that everything was in order and that he had not forgotten anything. Already Willy had most of the gear and food taken out of the truck and placed on the asphalt parking lot.

Impatiently, Willy exclaimed, "Hurry up, dad. You're going to make us late."

With a smile Mr. MacNeil looked at his son and replied, "Late for what, son? I don't know of any schedule that we drew up, do you? Anyway, I must be sure our chart is accurate and our route is marked out properly."

16

"Alright, dad, but hurry it up, ple-ea-a-s-e!" Willy begged with a sigh. "I want to go fishin'!" "Detail, details!" Willy thought to himself impatiently.

When the chart and route were double-checked, Willy and his dad carried the supplies and fishing gear from the parking lot down to the shore and out along the long wooden floating dock.

 The Wharves

At the very last "stall" on the dock was Arthur MacNeil's boat. Mr. MacNeil carefully stepped into the boat with some of their gear and supplies. His boat was painted white with a bright blue trim and lettering. On each side of the bow was printed the boat's name, THE MARINER. Willy paused to look at this boat before stepping on board. It seemed to be the finest boat he had ever seen. As he too stepped into the boat, Willy said to no-one in particular, "I bet this is the best boat in the whole world." Little did he know that he might not think so by the time this fishing trip was over.

Willy's dad had him take the lures and flashers that were used for commercial fishing out of the storage lockers. Mr. MacNeil went down below to the engine room through the hatch on the deck to check the engine oil and coolant levels. Then he climbed up the stairs to the deck to find that Willy had already set up three hand-operated downriggers that are used to lower the fishing lures down into deep water. As they were driving to the docks Mr. MacNeil had explained how they were to be fastened to the boat. He was pleased that Willy had done such a good job without being told to do it.

He complimented Willy with a big grin: ""Nice work, son. That will save us some time when we get to our fishing spot." Willy beamed with joy at the compliment. He always wanted to please his dad. His dad was away working so often that for long periods at a time he did not even get to see his father, let alone gain

18

his approval as much as he wanted. Besides, having the gear ready meant that he would be able to get fishing faster when they got to the area that they wanted to fish.

Both eager fishermen donned lifejackets. Willy's dad explained that they were not often worn by fishermen on commercial boats but they were necessary for safe boating even though the chances of having problems on a boat as big as his troller were not very likely. Mr. MacNeil wanted his son to learn safe practices right from the start. How important this would prove to be in a few hours.

Mr. MacNeil went into the cabin as Willy looked around at everything on the deck of the boat. Having checked everything in the cabin, Mr. MacNeil started the engine and all the gauges indicated that everything was in order and ready to go. The fuel tank was full of gasoline and the engine oil pressure was at the right level. He called to Willy to come into the cabin that was also their pilothouse. There Willy's dad prayed asking

19

God to protect them on their fishing trip. "Heavenly Father," he said, as if talking to an old friend, "thanks for this beautiful day and the good weather. Please keep us safe and give us a good fishing trip. Oh, yes, again I ask that you please take good care of Mom while we are gone. Thanks, Lord. In Jesus' name, Amen."

"Dad prays about everything!" Willy thought impatiently and a bit angrily. "He already prayed at breakfast. Why does he have to do it again?"

He wished that his dad would just cool it with that religion stuff but he knew enough not to say anything and get his dad upset. He was out here to have fun with his dad, not get religious! That was the one thing about his dad that really bugged him. His friends would sometimes make fun of the fact that Mr. MacNeil was always praying and sharing his faith in God. They made fun of him by calling him "The God Man". Mr. MacNeil would explain to people that since the Lord created them and provided for them, they should be grateful and let Him know. Willy

20

would always cringe with embarrassment when this happened. Willy would just as soon have his dad leave God out of their lives.

The last job before leaving the dock was to untie the boat from its moorings and guide it out from its position beside the dock. They needed to be careful that the boat would not hit either the dock or the fishing boat on the other side of their boat that was moored beside it. Willy eagerly untied the ropes, lifted up the rubber bumpers that they call "fenders" that are used to prevent the boat from rubbing against the dock or other boats, and tossed them onto the deck of their boat. On other occasions he had helped to untie the ropes and then watch his father and helper, sometimes with his mother, head out to sea while he had to stay behind. This time Willy had jumped on board and they were headed off for an exciting day of Pacific salmon fishing. He grinned with excitement to think that this time he was finally in the boat as well.

As the boat sped out towards their proposed fishing grounds, the area on the water where they planned to fish, Willy felt good that his dad trusted him to help with the boat. It was a big responsibility. He was sure that he would not disappoint his dad on this trip. He would be a good sailor. He would not get seasick. He would be a good fisherman and catch his fair share of the fish. He would be a real man that would certainly impress his dad! Would he ever have a lot to tell his friends when he got back! Would they ever be jealous of him! All of this passed through Willy's mind as the fishing boat slowly pulled into the bay out past the other boats that were moored nearby in the bay.

Willy looked back at the dock and his town nestled comfortably beneath the beautiful snow-capped mountains. He felt a strange twinge of longing to stay on shore. This was the first time that he had ever gone out of sight of his hometown. He sensed a warm feeling inside whenever he thought about his home. He loved

22

his little town of Eaglecrest. He hoped that he would always live there.

The boat was now travelling out with the tide at about thirty knots. Mr. MacNeil explained to Willy that it is much easier on the boat engine and is faster when the tide is moving in the same direction that the boat is travelling. If you are travelling against the flow of the tide it is harder on the engine and uses much more fuel. They were leaving at just the right time to make full use of the direction of the tidal flow.

The saltchuck looked beautiful. Seagulls seemed to be everywhere, some perched on posts sticking out of the water. Others flew this way and that searching for an early breakfast.

Willy remembered his dad telling him how a hungry seagull once grabbed a lure and got it caught in its beak. It flew upward until the line grew tight. It was the first time that the fishermen had to pull their catch out of the sky but they managed to pull it down to the boat. It was

23

a terrible fight as the frightened bird tried to get the hook free from its beak. One person had to hold the terrified bird as still as possible while the other one removed the hook. Once freed, the seagull flew off as fast as it could. Willy smiled as he thought, "I doubt if that seagull ever tried to catch a lure again. I wonder if dad thought he was catching a flying fish when the line went skyward."

Willy's thoughts returned to the trip they were taking and he noticed some seals diving from the rocks of a small island; they were after some fish, no doubt. They were pretty to watch but were a nuisance to the commercial fishermen, sometimes taking fish right off the lines as they were being pulled in. It was reported that some fishermen even carried shotguns on board their fishing vessels to kill the seals so they would not steal their catch. Even though the seals were a problem to the fishermen, Willy knew that his dad would not break the law and do anything like that.

Once in a while a large white-headed osprey, or "fish-hawk" as some people called them, would circle overhead and then plunge to the water below. It would swoop up from the water and climb skyward with a fish in its sharp talons. Sometimes the bird found it difficult to rise above the water as a large fish in its talons would flop this way and that and cause the osprey to almost fall to the ocean. Then, with a series of flaps of its strong wings the osprey would head for home with its precious catch.

"What a way to fish!" Willy exclaimed to his dad. "That's awesome! I wish I had brought a camera to take a picture of that bird catching his dinner."

"Yes, son, we'll have to bring a camera the next time we go fishing," replied Mr. MacNeil. "God has given these creatures special abilities to catch fish in their own way. We are not quite as gifted as the osprey, so we can't swoop down and catch fish as he does. God has given us minds, though, to think of how to outsmart some of those fish and catch them in our way. Even then a lot of fish get away. Bald eagles along the coast go fishing the same way."

25

Willy looked the other way and scowled. "Dad talks too much about God," he thought. "Ever since he got religious two years ago he's been a pain. He brings God into everything we talk about. Even my friends call him a fanatic. I can get along fine without God and I don't need Him to help me catch fish either. I'll catch my own fish my own way, thank you. I'll soon prove that!"

For some time after this, neither one spoke as they sped on. Willy did not want to say anything in case his dad might "get religious" on him again. Mr. MacNeil sensed the resentment in the way Willy was acting and so decided it was best to say nothing rather than get Willy upset any more. He had been praying for his son a great deal lately. Mr. MacNeil did not know how to show Willy how much God really loved him and how wonderful it is to know Jesus Christ as Saviour and Lord. His heart ached for his son to accept Jesus and discover His love for him but he wisely left the work of touching Willy's heart to the Holy Spirit. He had prayed just the previous

26

night that somehow God would reveal Himself to Willy and work in his life regardless of the cost. Mr. MacNeil hoped that the cost would not be as great as he feared it might have to be in order to reach Willy for God. Mr. MacNeil knew that sometimes it takes a disaster in order to cause some people to turn to the Lord Jesus Christ.

CHAPTER TWO: CHECKING THINGS OUT FOR

FISHING

Willy and his dad watched other boats out on the water. Some were pleasure boats and some were "working boats" as Willy's dad called them. There were tug boats, usually hauling barges loaded with vehicles, gravel, logs encircled by other logs tied together called a "boom" or other cargo, with long cables behind the boats. Some boats were commercial fishing boats of many sizes and types. Then there were the big British Columbia ferries that carried passengers from the mainland to the islands or Sunshine Coast.

Island after island appeared in their view to the west. Some were large and some were very small. Some had lighthouses on them and some were uninhabited, at least as far as they could see, with nothing but trees and grass on them.

The trip to where Mr. MacNeil and Willy were going was taking a long time. Willy began to be bored, even though he enjoyed the scenery. His dad sensed this. To kill some time he decided to try a quiz on his son that he had gone over many times with him before.

"Willy, how about we try our salmon quiz to see if you're up on your facts about them?"

"Sure, dad," Willy countered. "You can't get me on any of those questions. I know all the answers."

"Okay, then," replied his dad. "What are the names of the five varieties of Pacific salmon?"

"I got you on that one, dad. There are actually six now: sockeye, chinook, coho, chum, and the occasional Atlantic salmon that somehow got into the Pacific ocean."

"That's a bonus point for you, Willy," Mr. MacNeil exclaimed. "You're absolutely right! There used to be only five varieties of salmon on the Pacific coast but recently there have been some Atlantic salmon showing up here as well because of fish farmers who try to keep

29

them in their pens along the coast both in B.C. and Washington state. How did you know about them, Will?"

"I read it in the Fishing Guide, dad," Willy exclaimed proudly. "Gotta keep up on all the new regs and information."

"Right you are, son. Now, how about another question? What are silvers?"

"That's a trick question, dad. Cohos, especially young cohos, are often called silvers but there's a freshwater fish that's called silvers too," Willy said. "Ummm, let me see. I know what they are. Oh yeah, they are sockeyes that are in lakes and can't get out."

"That's right," Mr. MacNeil said. "They are found in landlocked freshwater lakes."

"Don't give me any clues," Willy begged. "I can remember. Just a minute! They are something like Coca-cola fish; no, Coke knees; no, I've got it, kokanees!"

30

"Right on. Whew, what an effort," Willy's dad exclaimed. "It was a bit of a trick question but you got the answer right. I'm pleased with you, son. That was a hard one."

Willy almost burst with pride. He was always happy when he made his dad happy. He thought, "This is gonna be a good day!"

"Now another question, Willy!" his dad continued. "How can you tell the difference between the Pacific salmon varieties."

"Oh, that's one's that is easy to get mixed up," Willy replied. "Ah, let me think. Let's see; I think the sockeye are very silvery-blue and are skinny compared to the other fish. When it's spawning time they turn red on the outside."

"We called that being slender or slim. They also have prominent glassy eyes. You're right so far," Willy's dad commented. "Why did you say, 'red on the outside'?"

31

"'Cause their meat is red all the time," Willy answered.

"Right again, Wild Will!" his dad replied. "What are the rest like?"

"Okay then, the coho have black tongues with white gums and have some spots on the top of their tails which are silvery but not on the bottom. Chum are lighter in colour and look something like sockeye but are thicker. They also have white tips on their back fins underneath."

"Right again, son," Mr. MacNeil commented. "By the way, that back fin underneath is called the anal fin. Continue on."

Willy continued, "Pinks have large oval spots on their tails which don't have any silver on them. They are silver with spots on their backs. In fact, they are covered with spots. Chinooks have black gums and silver tails with lots of spots on them. Their backs are bluish-green with a few spots on them. And that's that!"

32

"Excellent, Wild Will!" his dad exclaimed. "Now, one final question, "What other names are given to these salmons?"

"Okay," Willy answered, "Pinks are called humpbacks because they get big humps on their backs behind their heads when they spawn. Chum are sometimes called Keta or Silver Brite or dog salmon. Sockeyes are sometimes called Bluebacks or Reds. Chinook salmon are sometimes called Kings or Springs. How's that?"

"Right on, son," Mr. MacNeil replied. "By the way, do you know why chum are sometimes called 'dog salmon'?"

"Because they are so bad that only dogs will eat them?" Willy asked.

"Not really, They are not that bad for eating. They are called dog salmon because when they swim up the rivers to spawn they grow long teeth that look like a dog's fangs. Also you might not know that all salmon are good

33

for people with high cholesterol or who have heart disease. The oil in the meat helps to reduce bad cholesterol."

"Cool, dad! Not only does salmon taste good but it's good for you," Willy commented with a grin.

"Know why I give you the salmon quiz every so often?" his dad asked.

"I guess you want to keep me from getting bored," Willy answered.

"Not exactly although it helps; I want you to be able to distinguish between species because we are going for only one kind," Mr. MacNeil said.

"Right on, dad! Chinook! Springs! Kings!" Willy exclaimed.

They looked out at the scenery as they sped past, well at least as fast as they could go in a troller. Trollers are not known for their speed. Some dolphins followed them at a distance to the right, leaping into the air from time to time.

"Look, Wild Will, they are doing that on porpoise!" Mr. MacNeil shouted to Willy, who had just stepped out the cabin door to look over the rail at these beautiful creatures.

"Sick joke!" Willy shot back with a chuckle.

The boat had been travelling basically south along the coastline but now they changed direction.   Mr. MacNeil stooped over to look at the screen on the radar. There were a series of small islands to the right and Mr. MacNeil, without slowing down, turned the boat toward them heading west.   Willy almost panicked as the boat turned quickly and sped toward one of the small islands, thinking that they were not going to slow down and would hit the rocky shore.

He ran inside the cabin again and screamed, "We're gonna crash, dad!,"

Mr. MacNeil just smiled and said, "No we're not. It just looks that way.   Watch.   There's a channel up ahead"

35

In a few seconds, Willy saw a narrow channel that angled off to the right, not more than a quarter kilometre wide, into which they were going. Willy smiled sheepishly at his lack of trust in his dad. He felt foolish. His dad knew where they were going.

"Sorry, dad. I didn't see the channel."

"That's okay, Wild Will, you can't see it until you get up close. Life is like that, too. Sometimes things are going what looks like the wrong way and it looks as if you are going to crash. Then as time goes you see a channel for an escape route off to the side." Mr. MacNeil continued, "The Bible says that when we're up against a trial or temptation God won't allow us to be tested above what we can handle but with the testing will make a way of escape. Anyway, we're headed for the channel now so everything is okay."

Willy realised that he did not have to be afraid. Why, his dad knew this area like the back of his own hand. Willy had no reason not to trust his dad. His dad

36

had always come through for him. Little did Willy know that by the time this trip was over he would have learned a great deal more about trust.

Inside the channel, Mr. MacNeil slowed down slightly as he kept a trained eye watching for other boats and half-submerged logs. As they weaved back and forth with the channel that ran between the shorelines of several islands clustered together, Mr. MacNeil called out to Willy, "Watch out for deadheads, son."

"What in the world are deadheads, dad?" Willy asked.

"Oh, I forgot. You wouldn't know about them," Mr. MacNeil replied. "Deadheads are half-submerged logs that are sticking upright or on a slight angle in the water. Often they are just below the surface or you will see just the tip of them will sticking up. You have to look carefully to see them and if you hit one it could damage the boat badly; even sink it."

37

"Oh, okay," Willy answered. "I'll watch for them. You can count on me. I'll be a good deadhead watcher."

"Thanks, son," his dad replied with a smile. "I appreciate your help."

Willy peered out across the sparkling water searching for any deadheads that might be lurking out in the water in front of them. There was no sign of floating logs or deadheads anywhere in front of them but Willy kept careful watch. He did not want to see the boat damaged and anything bad happen to their fishing trip. This trip was too special to him.

Just as he began to get bored looking for danger, he spotted a deadhead just at the water's surface straight ahead. "Dad, there's a deadhead straight ahead of us", Willy yelled even though they were both inside the cabin together.

"Got ya," Mr. MacNeil said as he steered around it to the right. "When we see a deadhead straight ahead we say, 'Deadhead at 12 o'clock.' One off to the right is either one or two o'clock depending on its location, just like we are looking at the face of a clock."

"And dad, let me guess," Willy offered. "If I see one to the left it will be either ten or eleven o'clock, right?"

"You've got it, Wild Will," his dad answered.

As they continued along the channel they rounded the tip of a small island and in front of them a huge island loomed straight ahead, causing the channel to narrow and turn sharply towards the northwest.

"That island," Mr. MacNeil stated, "is called `Big Island' for obvious reasons. Once we get around the northern tip of Big Island we will be out in the open sea and near our fishing spot."

Willy grinned. He was too excited to speak. He could hardly wait to drop his line into the water. Willy looked at the hand-operated downriggers that he had put into place. His dad had explained that although the boat had motor-driven winches used commercially to carry the

39

many lines down to where the fish would be swimming it is illegal to use them when sport fishing. Everything was ready; Willy especially. In fact, Willy figured he had been ready all morning.

As the boat rounded the tip of Big Island, Willy saw the open sea for the first time. Up to that point the open sea had been hidden by the string of many islands that run parallel to the mainland. Now as far as he could see to the west was open water. They were where they wanted to be in order to fish.

CHAPTER THREE: A CHANGE OF PLANS

Mr. MacNeil slowed the boat down and put the propeller into neutral so that the boat would just drift slowly. Mr. MacNeil pointed to the area that in which he intended to fish and began to explain the course he would take. He told Willy that it was important to keep an eye on the islands as well as the instruments in the boat so they would know their location at all times. It is easy to lose track of where you are out in the open water.

Willy and his dad went to the back of the boa,t called the stern, to hook up their lines. Then his dad looked up at the ocean horizon. Mr. MacNeil's face took on a look of concern. Not too many miles to the north, big black clouds were gathering. He noticed that several other boats were already out fishing. Either they did not notice the storm clouds or they did not consider them as a serious threat. After all, the weather office had said that the bad storm that they had expected to hit the coast

41

would probably stay well to the north and not affect them at all in this location.

Storm Clouds Coming Over The Islands

Mr. MacNeil turned to Willy and said, "Son, we won't set out our lines right now. That storm looks like it is coming mighty fast. We will anchor in the mouth of the channel where it's shallower. We might be able to wait out the storm and then go fishing afterwards."

Willy had already noticed that the wind had risen sharply and white foam was bursting on the tops of the waves. Everyone in Eaglecrest knew that these whitecaps spelled some windy weather and often the

42

beginning of a storm. It felt cold as well. Willy sensed the seriousness of the situation and he began to feel raw fear gnawing inside him. Disappointed but eager not to get caught out in the coming storm, Willy agreed with his dad. He felt a little lump of fear in his throat as he replied, "Okay, let's go and see what happens, dad," Willy said.

"It could be just a short cloudburst, Willy," his dad said with more confidence and calmness than Willy felt as they headed into the mouth of the channel that they had just come from. "Let's get our raingear on and we will wait out the storm," Willy's dad added.

Willy felt better after his dad had shared his plans to anchor in the channel. Maybe the storm would pass and they would get to do some fishing after all. He helped his dad set the anchor after they had stopped in the channel mouth and had turned off the boat engine. Even as young as he was, Willy knew that they would receive some shelter from the wind with the little island

43

between them and the coming storm. He felt better being close to the island. Somehow being close to some land made him feel better in case something bad happened. They looked up and saw that the other boats in the area were also speeding for the shelter of nearby bays to get out of the fury of the storm.

Then the storm hit fiercely. It came fast. It hit hard. It struck the boat with gale force winds, causing it to bounce on the high waves like a cork on the rapids of a fast-flowing creek. This was a vicious storm, much worse than either of them had expected.

"Well," thought Mr. MacNeil, "we had not planned on this but we'll soon find out if Willy has the makings of a good sailor."

It was a good thing that they had anchored in the channel. Although the boat was being tossed around in the channel, the waves out at the fishing spot were now being whipped up two and three metres (six to ten feet) high. Although the troller was seaworthy, the tossing

44

waves would have shaken things up badly and possibly caused Willy to become very seasick and maybe injured.

The rain came down in sheets so that it became almost impossible to see the shore of Big Island. In fact, all they could see clearly was the side of the channel next to which they were anchored. It was a huge black cliff reaching up into the darkness of the falling rain. Even with his dad standing beside him, Willy felt a wave of loneliness and fear sweep over him with every bit as much turmoil as the salty waves outside the boat.

Mr. MacNeil hollered, "Stay here, Willy. I'll be right back." Then he hurried to batten down the hatches securely and make sure that things on the deck were reasonably secure. Before Willy had time to think much about the storm his dad came running back into the cabin to join him to escape the wind and the rain. They held on to the shelf that ran around the cabin and watched the unbelievable wildness of the storm. At times

45

they could not even see past the bow of the boat in the heavy rainfall as the storm increased.

"I never expected this, Wild Will," Mr. MacNeil said almost apologetically.

"That's okay, Dad," Willy replied with an uneasy grin. "This is an adventure. Besides, I see clear sky behind the clouds to the north. This will soon be over and then we can go fishing." Sure enough, a shaft of sunlight pierced through the clouds behind the storm.

No sooner had Willy finished talking than a huge wave lifted them upward and then pushed the boat up and over on its port side. The boat came down in the wave's trough with a crash on its starboard side and then the wave subsided. The boat righted itself almost immediately.

Both Willy and his dad had been taken off guard. They had crashed against the cabin wall. Loose items in the cabin had been flung to the floor. They had kept some fishing gear in the cabin that was now scattered on the floor but they were not sure what had been lost overboard out on the deck of the boat.

"Are you alright, son?" Mr. MacNeil asked his son worriedly as he dabbed at a small bleeding gash on his own forehead.

"Yeah. I think so. I'm scared dad. I'm not really hurt, but your head's bleeding. Are you gonna be okay?" Willy asked.

"I'm fine. This gash is just a small cut and it will heal fast," he assured his son as he looked into a small mirror that had fallen to the floor but had not broken. Then he turned his thoughts to their situation. "I've never been hit broadside with a wave like that before in the open water. I hope the boat is alright. I guess the wave came in so high because the channel is shallow here and the wave had no direction to go but up."

The two of them just stood there clinging to the cabin ledge as they tried to calm down from the severe shaking they had just endured. Then suddenly the squall

47

ended as quickly as it had come and within minutes the water smoothed off. However, more black clouds were forming on the distant horizon.

Mr. MacNeil turned to Willy and said, "Son, I am sorry to tell you this but another storm is coming. I think we had better check out the boat to be sure that it is not damaged, pull anchor and then head for home. I guess our fishing will have to wait for another day."

"But Dad," Willy protested, "that storm is a long ways away. Couldn't we just fish for a few minutes and when the storm gets closer then pack it in? We've come a long way and we haven't put even one lure in the water. At least we could say that we tried to do some fishing for at least a few minutes. Can't we, Dad, ple-ea-a-se! Can't we go fishing?"

Mr. MacNeil looked at his son grimly. He could see disappointment etched on his young face. He so much did not want to disappoint his son. Giving in to Willy's plea, against his better judgement, Mr. MacNeil

48

said, "Well, okay. But just for a few minutes, and then we'll go home, Wild Will, or we might have a bigger adventure than we really want." How true these words would prove to be, Mr. MacNeil did not really know at that moment.

Experience at sea had taught Mr. MacNeil that this action was not wise. His training said that it was a mistake. In fact everything inside him told him it was not a good move to go back out to the ocean to fish. However, he did not want to let down this boy who had longed for this trip for so many weeks. He shook his head at his own decision, wondering if he was doing what was right, as Willy let out a whoop of happiness and ran to raise the anchor.

CHAPTER FOUR: DISASTER AT SEA

The sea had returned to relative calm once again in spite of the dark clouds to the north. Mr. MacNeil started the engine and headed out towards the fishing spot. He pushed forward on the throttle to gain speed but the engine did not rev up. In fact, it spluttered and then began to idle roughly.

"Oh, no," he said. "Something must have been damaged when that big wave hit us."

"I'll go check," Willy shouted as he unbattened the hatch to the engine room, even though he did not know what he was looking for. As he lifted the hatch, he yelled to his father, "Dad, I smell gas! Stop the engine! Quick!" The engine room was full of gasoline fumes. Willy knew that gasoline fumes are dangerously explosive. He stepped back as he shouted. It was a good thing.

Mr. MacNeil could not react fast enough. Before he could shut down the engine, a spark somewhere in the engine compartment ignited the gasoline fumes. There was a tremendous explosion. Although Willy had stepped back from the hatch a few feet, the explosion surged through the open hole, blew his hat off, set his clothes on fire and blew him out of the boat into the salty water. Had Willy been looking into the hatch the explosion would surely have killed him. The blast also blew a section of the starboard side right out of the boat and shattered all of the windows on board. As the boat began to quickly sink, Mr. MacNeil dove out of the broken cabin window into the churning sea, now being swirled around by the increasing wind from the approaching storm.

When Willy hit the water, the fire on his clothes was quickly extinguished by the salty water. He surfaced, coughing and gasping for breath, tasting only salt. His face was slightly burned and the salt water caused his injuries to sting, but no bones were broken as far as he could tell. He was sore from the impact of the blast and the impact of hitting the water but he was alive and well; at least as well as any person could be in that situation. In fact, although Willy did not know it, the salt water was helping to destroy any infection that might have resulted from his injuries.

All Willy could think about was where his dad was and he yelled as loud as he could, "Dad, Dad"! Then the storm that Willy had thought was so far away suddenly hit the area with all the force it could muster. Pieces of the burning boat were being tossed by angry waves. The pelting rain made it impossible to see ahead more than half a metre ahead (a couple of feet). Willy could not see his dad because of the high waves and the rain. He called out for his dad over and over but the roar of the storm drowned out his words. He grasped for a broken plank floating nearby to hold on to in order to stay steady.

Clinging to the plank, Willy began to cry for the first time in many months. He had decided that he was not a cry baby and was too old to cry. However, he could

52

not contain his emotions and he cried loudly. Between sobs he would scream for his dad as loudly as he could. He had once decided that he would be Mr. Tough Guy. All had changed with the storm surging around him. Now he imagined his dad floating lifelessly in the sea. Fear and guilt overwhelmed him.

Bobbing up and down on the water in the pelting rain, Willy screamed out over and over, "Dad, where are you? Dad, answer me. Dad, Dad!" His voice finally began to get hoarse and he realised that if his dad was alive, the storm was drowning out his voice and his dad would not hear him anyway. He stopped screaming and began to cry as he grabbed at a bigger piece of wood floating in the water to better stay afloat.

"It's all my fault," he sobbed hoarsely. "If I hadn't wanted to fish so much, Dad might have checked the engine room before starting the engine instead of trying to beat the storm. A big sailor I am! I can't do anything right. I tried to be a big tough guy! I didn't think I needed

53

anybody. I said I don't need God. I sure need somebody. God, if You're really there, I need you big time right now", he yelled through the storm. "Help me God, please!" This was a cry of desperation as Willy was tossed back and forth among the debris from the sinking boat.

Floating in his charred raingear and lifejacket, grasping a floating broken plank, bouncing up and down on the wild waves of the storm in the saltchuck and half blinded by the pouring rain, Willy remembered telling his dad that he did not want to go back to Sunday School anymore. This made him think of the reason why. His Sunday School teacher, Mrs. Blaine had said, "Children," (that irked him because he did not liked to be called a child. After all he was nine now, not a baby), "Sometimes we think we can do everything on our own. We think we don't need God. In fact, the Bible says, `All we like sheep have gone astray; We have turned every one to his own way'. Everyone of us has been rebellious towards God and has chosen to do wrong. This is called "sin". As a

54

result, all of us are condemned to that horrible punishment called "hell' because, `The wages of sin is death', the Bible says. We cannot save ourselves. Our sins separate us from God who loves us and wants to be our loving Father. The Bible says that is why Jesus, God's Son, came. He gave up His life on the cross. He took our sins and our punishment for our sins on Himself. He did not earn punishment for His own sins for He never did wrong. Therefore, when He died, Jesus took the punishment that we earned, death for our wrongs. He died for each person who ever would be born afterwards. If we ask God for forgiveness, believe in Jesus and ask Him to be our Saviour, He will save us and we will become God's children. Then we will have an eternal home in heaven, the Bible says. You must make the choice to accept Jesus as your own Saviour. No-one else can do it for you. It is something that each one of us must do for ourselves. Is there anyone who would like to receive Jesus as their Saviour today?"

55

At that time Willy had thought, "No way! I don't care what the Bible says. I don't need God. I get too much of that from mom and dad already. That's for sissies and old religious people but not for me." Now it was different. Willy needed God now and he needed Him badly. Now he was glad that his mom and dad had made him go to Sunday School to hear about the love of Jesus.

Hoping that God could hear him through the noise of the storm, Willy called upward to God. "God, I said I didn't need You but I was so wrong! I need You to help get me out of this mess. I need You to forgive me. Please forgive me, God. Jesus , please be my Saviour. I believe in You. I really do, just as the Bible says. Save me, God. God, just help me get out of this mess. Help me to get out of this and I'll do whatever You want. Please help me and my dad too." Not knowing what else to say, Willy finished with, " Amen."

Although the storm was raging all around Willy and he was being tossed all around in the water, a

56

strange inner peace settled inside him. The storm inside him had amazingly disappeared. He realised that God had indeed heard him in spite of the noise of the storm. Willy knew that for the first time in his life that he was right with God. Whatever happened to him from now on did not really seem to matter for he was in God's loving care.

Yes, the fear of his situation was real. Willy knew he was still in danger. He was terrified that something bad had happened to his dad. He was sore and in pain from the burns he had experienced. He was scared of what could happen to him physically but he knew that He was right with God. Regardless of what happened he was now in God's hands and His care.

CHAPTER FIVE: ADVENTURES WITHOUT DAD

The wind had calmed briefly. Willy looked up and saw a couple of sharp fins that looked like triangles sticking out of the water. They were at the other side of the channel but they were slowly weaving back and forth, coming his way. "Oh no", he hollered as loud as his hoarseness would allow, "Sharks!"

Like everyone else along the Pacific coast Willy had heard of shark attacks. Although sharks seldom attack people, several people had survived shark attacks suffering severe bites. According to the commercial fishermen a couple of others had been torn to pieces by the sharp teeth on these fish. He had seen shark attacks in the movie theatre and fear gripped him. Suddenly all the fins turned and began to come straight toward him. Fear grew and engulfed him. He tried to think about what he had heard to do if such a thing should ever happen to him.

Willy tried to lay flat on the water. He knew that thrashing around in the water would only attract the sharks to him, especially with the burns and cuts that he had received from the explosion, and then he would probably become a fast lunch for them. He turned his head to get a better look at the fins coming his way. As he did something very hard bumped against the back of his head. He turned over in the water as best as his life-jacket would allow and could not believe his eyes. There, floating in the waves beside him was an old wooden rowboat. It was a small boat that had seen better days but it was floating. Willy thought it looked something like a wooden lifeboat, a boat that is used as a rescue boat on a bigger boat, to save the lives of people from a sinking ship in the ocean, but it was too small to be one. Willy took one quick glance at the fins now zeroing in on him. Terrified, he grabbed the edge of the boat and quickly hauled himself up and into the boat without tipping it far enough to let the ocean water in. As Willy

59

sat up, the sharks bumped against the boat hard. Several times the sharks hit the boat. Then realizing that they had lost their prey, the sharks swam away.

Willy looked around as he sat in his new-found boat bouncing around in the gale. There were about fifteen centimetres (six inches) of water in it but he could stay out of the water by sitting on its middle seat with his feet tucked under him. There was what looked like a big first aid box in the stern, but there were no oars. He would have to let the boat drift wherever it would be driven by the winds, waves and ocean currents. Even if there had been oars, Willy was too tired and sore to try to use them.

Now that Willy was safe from the danger of sharks he could consider other matters. All at once Willy began to think about what had happened. Where was his dad? Had he been injured? Had he drowned? Had the sharks gotten him? Willy began to scream again as loudly as his sore throat would let him as tears ran down his cheeks,

"Dad! Dad! Where are you?" Over and over Willy called out but the wind had picked up again and the noise of the raging storm drowned out his words or the words of any possible response. With his voice growing even hoarser, Willy stopped shouting.

Finding his sitting position difficult after being in the kneeling position for a while, especially with the boat tossing up and down and back and forth in the storm, Willy moved to the rear seat. He leaned his head against the stern and stretched out so that just his feet were in the water in the boat. As he began to cry again he drifted off to sleep as the raging storm around him picked up in intensity. Rain poured down around him and into the boat as well. Willy was a very sad, frightened and extremely weary boy.

Willy's sleep was fitful. He dreamed about boat wrecks, fires, disasters and horrible storms, as well as terrifying sea creatures. From time to time he would awaken with a start from his nightmares, frightened as

61

the storm raged on around him. It was then that he would tearfully call out to God asking for God to protect his dad and somehow rescue him. Then he would sleep and dream some more.

Finally, Willy awoke. The storm had lifted. The sky was bright with fluffy white cumulus clouds dotting the sky. He looked around to find himself drifting along an unfamiliar shore on the starboard side. A range of islands kept the ocean to the port side out of sight.

Willy did not know how long he had been asleep. He had no idea where he was. It was obvious that the storm was long past and he was hungry. There were about thirty centimetres (a foot) of water in the bottom of the boat now. He decided to look inside the box in the stern to see if there might be some type of food there. He found some first aid supplies, matches in an air tight container, fishing lures, fishing line and some sinkers, but no food.

"I might as well try fishing," Willy said to himself. "After all, that's why I came out here in the first place, and besides, I have to get something to eat. I'm starving."

The ocean was fairly calm now, rippling with a gentle breeze. Willy tied a shiny lure to the end of some fishing line as best as he could. He knotted the line, just as his dad had shown him, three times to be sure it was snug. The lure he chose had a pink and white plastic skirt that looks something like a small squid. He didn't know it then but it is a common fishing lure on the Pacific coast called a Hoochie. He attached a heavy lead sinker farther up the line, just as his dad had taught him the week before. Then he dropped the line with its tackle over the side of the boat. He had heard that salmon like to follow a slow troll. Drifting along in a gentle breeze would be about as slow as you could get in trolling. He grinned when he thought of that.

Then Willys thought, "I hope it is not too slow or I might end up catching a dogfish and the last thing I want

63

to do is to bring in any of those things aboard." Willy had heard his dad tell about these small sharks along the coast they called "dogfish". Although they don't seem to bother man, they do have sharp teeth and can contain high levels of mercury in their meat if they are over sixty centimetres (two feet) long. Therefore, most people don't eat them.

Willy wrapped the free end of the line several times around his left hand so that he would not lose the fish if he caught one. He said a quick prayer: "God, please help me catch a fish 'cause I'm sure hungry, in Jesus' name, Amen."

Drifting along, Willy's mind kept going back to the explosion, the sharks and his dad. He would cry softly and then ask God to take care of his dad and him too. At times loneliness, sadness and fear would overcome him and his whole body would shake with his sobs. For a while he would feel better and he would thank God for the nice weather and for saving his life. Then he would think about his family and his circumstances and cry some more.

After what seemed like hours to Willy the fishing line suddenly went slack. He thought that he had lost the sinker or lure so he started to quickly pull in the line. A quick jerk on the line almost pulled him out of the boat. It also convinced him that there was a fish on the end of the line. He did not realise that often a salmon will take the lure or bait and swim towards the fisherman in order to sample the bait. If the fish does not like it, he will spit out the lure and swim away. Coho will do it with such speed that it is virtually impossible to keep the line tight. Willy was fortunate that this fish was well hooked. As the fish pulled and jumped, the fishing line around Willy's hand pulled tight. His left hand started to hurt badly and he winced with pain. He wanted to let go of the fishing line but because it was wrapped so tightly around his hand he could not. Just when he thought he could stand the pain no longer, Willy felt the fish slacken off. The fish

65

was beginning to tire. He pulled the line in and brought the salmon beside the boat. When the fish saw the boat it dove downwards but Willy was able to easily pull the tired salmon back to and into the boat. Judging from the fish that his dad brought home on his troller, Willy figured that this one was a spring salmon weighing about two pounds.

Willy took the hook out of the fish's mouth and it began to swim around in the water in the boat. Willy laughed with joy and excitement. He was hooked on fishing now. He thought, "Catching that fish was a cinch. I'm going to catch another one."

He dropped the line into the water again, forgetting the fishing line burns on his hand. The sun was beginning to lower toward the horizon. Then something huge surfaced about three hundred metres (yards) away. A big, shiny, black and white creature arched out of the water and dove downward with a big splash of its wide-forked tail immediately after the first splash. Willy was thrilled although a bit anxious about being so close to such a large creature. He was viewing one member of a pod of killer whales, also called 'orca', swimming up the coast. Then he counted at least six whales, arching up out of the water in a spectacular diving performance. They were not coming any closer so he decided there was no danger to him and his little boat.

Willy looked toward the shore. He was drifting quickly towards a beach. He pulled in his empty fishing lure and put it back in the first aid box with the rest of the tackle. It was doubtful that there would be any fish nearby after the killer whales had come so close. Anyway, he was drifting into shore and had no way to change the direction of the boat. He hoped to get to shore and pull the boat up on to a nice beach. Besides that, it was getting late and he needed to eat some food and get shelter and Willy was all alone.

CHAPTER SIX: GIVE THANKS FOR ALL THINGS

As soon as the boat's bow touched the shore, Willy jumped out and pulled on the boat to bring it up on the sandy shore. He was glad to be on solid ground again. The sandy shore was littered with stones and larger rocks so he had a hard time pulling the boat out of the water but he kept trying. He pulled the boat as far as his limited strength allowed, out of the reach of the waves. Since the ocean was at high tide he knew from experience by living along the British Columbia coast that the water would not come any higher and float his rescue craft away. His boat would be safe there beached up on the shore.

The Abandoned Boat

Willy tried to walk along the beach. He wavered back and forth. He felt as if he was still moving up and down with the waves even though he was on solid ground. He was experiencing a common effect of being out in a boat for a long time. Not only do landlubbers need to get their "sea-legs" when going out on a boat in the ocean but sailors need to get their "land-legs" when getting back from a long trip on the water. Soon Willy was back to walking normally so he decided to look his landing spot over.

The Lonely Shore Looking Out At The Islands

The beach was only about one hundred and fifty metres (400 feet) long. It was a mixture of sand and rocks and someone had built a fire pit by making a circle or stones and burning some pieces of wood in it about halfway down the beach. Along the back of the beach was a fairly steep ridge about five metres (fifteen feet) high that followed the coastline. It was forested quite heavily in cedar, fir, hemlock and pine. Some alders and willows grew in patches up the grassy slope.

Willy climbed up the ridge and found a flat, treeless area there in front of him. Someone had cleared enough trees to make a sizeable campsite a long time ago. The cold, black remains of a campfire were near the middle of the cleared-off area. It looked as though tents had been set up around the campfire at one time as the grass had been flattened in small rectangular patterns. Off to the left was an old, dirt four-by-four trail, but the tire tracks were now washed out. Behind this cleared-off area

70

was a mossy slope leading up about six metres (twenty feet) into the thick forest beyond.

Then Willy went back down the ridge to the beach. As he came down, he noticed a white plastic object over to his right. He walked over to it and to his surprise discovered it to be a piece of plastic pipe driven horizontally into a freshwater spring in the ridge. Fresh ice-cold mountain water trickled out of the pipe. He leaned over and took a much needed drink. It was so refreshing! He washed his face and hands in the cold water and then stood up. Turning toward the ridge Willy saw some wild blackberry bushes laden with sweet, ripe fruit just above the plastic pipe. These huge black berries are much bigger than blackcap raspberries and when fully ripe are extremely sweet. Willy picked a handful of these berries and stuffed them into his mouth. How juicy and satisfying they were to this hungry boy.

For a moment Willy stopped and stood amazed at all of this. He did not know where he was, and he did not

71

know how he would ever get home, if he would at all, yet here was all that he would need for now to take care of his needs. Tears of gratitude welled up in his eyes as he began to thank God for taking care of him.

"Father," Willy humbly and reverently said as he prayed, "I know that I was Your lost son like the story of the Prodigal Son in Sunday School, but You found me today. You saved me from the explosion. You saved me from the sharks. You saved me from sin and You saved me from the storm. Now You've given me fish to eat, water to drink, a place to rest for the night, matches for a fire and berries for dessert. Thank You, Lord. I sure don't deserve it but dad was right. You sure do care for Your kids. Not only that, I haven't been good at trusting You; almost like I nearly didn't trust my dad when he was driving the boat, and yet I should've known better. You're awesome, God, and I really mean it! O yeah," he added sadly, "please take care of Dad if He's still alive and help me to get home. Please be with Mom and my friends and don't let them worry too much about me. Thank you, God, Amen."

Then Willy had a sudden thought. "Oh, man! Now I'm starting to talk like my dad. Oh well, I guess that is not too bad."

Willy did not have time to worry or cry now. He had to work fast. The sun was beginning to set, making a beautiful crimson sky. Willy remembered an old saying, "Red sky at night, sailor's delight; red sky in the morning, sailors take warning. I wonder if the sky was red this morning. I was too excited to notice." He knew that he had to cook the fish or he would have to eat it raw, something he did not like to think about.

He quickly gathered as much dry grass and wood as he could. He looked under any place that might have sheltered twigs and branches from the rain. He looked under trees, shrubs and the overhangs of big rocks. Then he gathered bigger pieces of wood. He put the

73

grass, the tiny, dry twigs and the bigger pieces of wood in a pile beside the fire pit that he had seen earlier.

Willy went over to the boat to get his fish. The salmon was not swimming very much because most of the oxygen in the water had been used up by its gills. In fact, the fish was close to death. Willy grabbed the fish and pulled it out of the boat and taking a large stone, hit the salmon between the eyes hard to kill it and keep it from suffering anymore. With the fish now dead, Willy had to clean it. He had seen his mom and dad do that many times so he knew what to do.

That morning before leaving home, Willy had hooked his filleting knife on to his belt. It was still in the sheath at his side so he removed it and began to clean the fish. After the fish had been cleaned and washed, Willy took it over to where the fire was. He looked at the fire and thought, "I can't put the fish on the fire to cook it or it will burn up. If only I had a steel sheet or something

74

to reflect heat from the fire down to where the fish is. Then the heat from the fire might cook the fish."

Suddenly Willy had an idea. He did not know if it would work but he was hungry and it was worth a try. He found a flat rock that he put on the gravel near the fire pit. Then he placed a tall rock with a fairly flat side across from the first rock with the flat side angled slightly toward the flat rock. Willy placed some dry grass in the area between the two rocks, then put on some twigs and then larger pieces of wood that he had found. He had seen his dad do this when they were camping once and he hoped it would work for him. He lit one match from the first aid box and put it to the base of the dry grass and twigs and they caught fire. Soon the wetter bigger twigs were sizzling and then blazing. The fire was hot enough to dry the small pieces of wood and start them burning as well as the twigs. To his delight Willy saw the fire was burning brightly. The large upright rock reflected the heat of the fire on to the other rock where Willy then placed the fish.

Since there was no breeze blowing by now, most of the fire's heat did reflect down on the fish. Willy did not realise it, but he had just made an excellent crude wilderness broiler. It is amazing what you can think of when you are forced to come up with something to save your life especially if you are extremely hungry.

As he waited for the fish to cook, Willy found a small driftwood branch shaped like the letter Y, to turn the fish so that it would cook evenly. It became his two pronged fork. He thought that it looked a lot like the holders used in rowboats to hold oars in place, called "oarlocks". Soon the salmon was cooked to what looked like perfection. He pulled it toward the cooler part of the flat rock on which it lay. After thanking God for the fish, Willy ate about half of it and then he had had enough. Nothing had ever tasted better to him. The fish was delicious!

Willy knew that he would need something for breakfast so he put some green sticks under the remaining piece of fish on the flat rock. He placed a large piece of cedar bark on the big rock so it would hang over the fire somewhat and direct the smoke downwards toward the fish. Then he put a bundle of green alder branches on the fire. The smoke belched up, curled around by the overhead piece of bark and circled downward to the fish before dissipating into the air. He had gotten the idea from watching his dad smoke fish in their smoker at home. Willy's home-made wilderness smoker was not perfect but it would smoke the fish well enough that the fish would not go bad overnight.

While the fish was being smoked, Willy climbed the ridge and began to make a temporary shelter out of cedar and fir branches around the base of a big cedar tree. It was not fancy but Willy hoped it would keep out most of the rain if another storm came. He and some friends had made a similar "wigwam", as they called it, during the summer holidays the year before. A few soft fir branches would relieve the ground of its hardness and make a bed so that sleeping would be better than on the hard ground. The shelter looked good but it is doubtful if the branches were dense enough to keep out a real storm if one came.

As darkness was settling in, Willy went down to the blackberry bushes and quickly ate another large handful of berries, being careful to avoid the large, sharp thorns on the bushes. He had experienced the pain of getting blackberry thorns in his legs and arms before and was not going to allow that to happen this time. Then he drank some water and rinsed out his mouth. It was the best he could do since he had no toothbrush or toothpaste with him. He took some of the fishing line from the boat and tied the smoked salmon from a high limb of a tree on the ridge so that predators could not get at it. He chose a tree far from his shelter for this purpose in case the fish might attract a hungry bear.

Willy checked to be sure that the fire was out. Then he washed his face and hands and headed for his shelter. He put his life jacket under his head for a pillow. His rain gear ensured that he would be warm and dry even if it was slightly charred from the explosion of the boat. Had anyone been standing nearby, they would have heard a very tired voice mumble, "Heavenly Father, thanks for everything. Thanks..." The weary young fellow could stay awake no longer.

Willy's Outdoor Fish Roaster

CHAPTER SEVEN: A NEW DAY

Morning comes early in the late summer forest in British Columbia. Willy woke up to the sound of what seemed like thousands of birds. Little sparrows hopped around chirping merrily. There was a curious flicker, an American goldfinch, and even a varied thrush. Songbirds of many kinds warbled and sang all around him. A couple of Canada Jays, commonly called "Grey Jays" or "Whiskeyjacks", fluttered around the campsite, hoping to find some food to scavenge. Big black shiny ravens at the top of a nearby pine tree squawked at each other and at times would call out their one melodious note that sounded like the ringing of a bell. The sound of the waves lapping at the shore drifted up to him calling him to rise and enjoy the new day before him. Hungry seagulls could be heard calling from somewhere above the shoreline.

Speaking of hungry, Willy suddenly remembered the smoked fish. He had hung it up to keep it away from animals on the ground. He had not even considered what birds could do to it if they found it. He looked out of his shelter to find his worse fears being enacted out before him. A raven was sitting on a cedar branch gobbling up the biggest part of the smoked salmon which he had torn loose from the rest of the suspended fish. A myriad of other kinds of birds were tearing at the remains of the salmon. A herring gull ripped the last piece of the fish from the fishing line and was happily flying away with its trophy. Two other gulls and a raven were dive-bombing the victor to try to make him drop his precious piece of salvaged breakfast. All of the loose bits of pieces of fish that had broken off in the process and fallen to the ground were being snatched up by several friendly Canada Jays and a couple of neighbourhood red squirrels.

Willy rushed out of his shelter at them waving his arms wildly. "Get out of here, you Gorbies!" he shouted. Willy had heard a visitor from New Brunswick call Canada Jays, "Gorbies" once. He felt that name sounded like a good insult to the camp robbers. The jays just flew up to some high branches to enjoy their breakfast, not perturbed in the least. A beautiful deep blue Stellar's Jay, British Columbia's official provincial bird, hopped up from some leaves and flapped across the campsite to safety.

Willy cried out, "Oh, no! What am I going to do now?" Then he did something that he had seen his dad do before on such frustrating occasions, though back then he could not understand it. He looked heavenward and with a grin shouted, "Praise the Lord anyhow!" It did not get the fish back but somehow praising God made Willy feel better.

Remembering the Lord now, Willy took time to talk to God, even as a pang of loneliness gripped him and brought tears to his eyes. "Heavenly Father, I'm glad

82

you're here with me or I'd be really all alone. Thank you for this bright and cheery day. I had a real good sleep. Did you? Oh, I forgot. Mrs. Blaine said that the Bible says that You never slumber or sleep. What's the difference between slumbering and sleeping? Anyway, Lord, we have a new day before us and I don't know what to do or how to get home. Lord, ple-ea-a-se help me. And oh, I know I should read the Bible but I don't have one so could you just pop a verse or two into my mind that I heard at Sunday School or church? Mrs. Blaine says that Christians should read the Bible and pray every day. If you make me remember what the Bible says then I will be able to think about that part of your Word. Thanks God. Amen."

A portion of a Scripture reading that Mrs. Blaine had shared in Sunday School class two weeks before came to his mind, at least parts of it. 1 Corinthians 15:1-4 was the reading. The parts that Willy could remember were: "...the gospel which I preached...by which also you

83

are saved...that Christ died for our sins according to...Scriptures...He was buried...He rose again the third day..." "I wish I could remember the whole thing," he thought, "but that's what I believed when I asked God to save me yesterday." God seemed very close to Willy at that moment and he felt as if he was wrapped up in the warmth of God's love.

Willy suddenly remembered that it was Sunday. "Today is the Lord's Day. I should be careful to honour God today," Willy thought out loud. "I want to obey Him every day, but shouldn't His day always be special?" he pondered. "I wonder why most Christians don't seem to love the Lord Jesus enough to treat His day special? Jesus did so much for me when He saved me I would think that everyone would love God so much that they would want to treat Him special and make His day special."

Hunger pangs told Willy that he could use some breakfast. He hurried down to the wild blackberry

84

bushes. He ate several handfuls and then drank his fill of ice-cold spring water. Thanking the Lord for something to eat and drink, Willy hurried down to the rocky beach.

Willy had some work to do. He wanted to be able to row the wooden boat through the water. He had it all figured out. He searched the shore until he found some beached wood suitable to make into a pair of oars. Since the two pieces were long, skinny and flat, only a small amount of carving was needed to make them suitable for rowing. That was good. A filleting knife has a slender pointed blade and is not designed for carving. Using one in this manner is hard on the blade's edge and can be dangerous if not done carefully. Willy figured that out and so was extra cautious so as not to cut himself or break the blade of his knife.

Willy remembered the Y-shaped piece of wood that he had used to flip the salmon on his broiler the night before. It had reminded him of oarlocks that are used to hold oars in place on a boat so that a person can row successfully. Willy went over to the grassy ridge and cut off two thirty centimetre (one-foot) lengths from green alder branches shaped like the letter Y. Some real carving was needed now. He took the pieces to the boat. He carved away most of the bottom fifteen centimetres (six inches) from each piece until they were pegs small enough to fit into the two oarlock holes in the boat when tapped down with a rock.

   After removing the first aid box on to the beach Willy pushed the boat over on its side as far as he could and let the water pour out onto the sand. The boat fell back on to its bottom when he let go of it. Then he climbed inside the boat with the new homemade oars. He sat with his back toward the bow in the rowing position. He set the newly carved oars into the V portion of the Y shaped oarlocks. Then Willy cut two lengths of fishing line and tied the oars to the oarlock pegs, wrapping the line around several times to ensure they were strong enough to hold the oars in place. He hoped that he had tied them well enough. Although this arrangement was rugged and crude, Willy now had a rowboat that he could propel and steer through the water.

Willy knew that he would have to fish again if he was going to get a proper meal to eat. There was nothing else to eat besides berries, birds and squirrels. He did not have the desire to kill a squirrel and the birds were too fast for him to catch. He needed to catch more fish.

The tide was out now. The boat had to be pulled or pushed to the water's edge. This was no small task for a boy. It was difficult but Willy slowly rocked and pushed the boat along. On the way to the water's edge he saw many clams and even some oysters but he dared not eat them. The deadly "red tide", a poisonous algae which turns the water rusty red, is a threat all along the west coast. Although the red tide was no longer there, the shellfish would remain poisoned for several years. Since it is always necessary to check with fisheries authorities to find out which shellfish at what locations are good to

87

eat, Willy did not dare take a chance. Everyone living along the coast knew about this and so he understood the danger of doing something so foolish.

When the boat was finally in the water, Willy sat on the seat facing the stern and tried rowing out to deeper water. It took a while but finally he learned how to manipulate the oars so that the boat would move forward properly. The water was almost as smooth as glass so rowing was quite easy for him. Then he dropped the lure and sinker overboard. This time, however, Willy tied the loose end of the fishing line to the seat of the boat in front of him. He had learned his lesson from the first fish that he had caught. He did not want to cut his hand with the fishing line this time.

A long time passed without a fish biting. The sun was up and the weather was warm. Since everything was so calm and there was no action on his lure, Willy had time to do some thinking. He began to realise that something had happened to him that had truly changed his life. He was not angry or upset or even as frightened as he would have been just a few days before. Instead, a strange comfortable peace gave him the confidence that everything would be fine for God was with   him."

So that's what Pastor Benson meant in his sermon last Sunday. He read from the Bible, `...if anyone is in Christ he is a new creation; old things have passed away; behold, all things have become new." This certainly had been true for Willy. All of his life seemed better even though the circumstances surrounding him appeared to be hostile and doomed for certain failure in the long run. In spite of his loneliness and concern about being lost and his dad's fate, Willy found a new happiness inside that he could not simply explain. Sure there were tears of concern and loneliness but things were not as bad as before Willy had accepted Christ for he knew that the Lord was with him at all times.

89

A jerk on the line brought Willy's attention back to the boat and what he was doing. Obviously a fish had taken the lure. Willy rowed just enough to keep the line tight. When the line tightened and began to put a lot of pressure backwards on the boat, he would slow down his rowing. When the line began to go slack, Willy would row faster. This kept the fish on the end of the line struggling until it tired itself out. Finally it seemed that the fish was just dragging along. Willy stopped rowing and carefully brought in the salmon. It was big enough to be legal for a sports fisherman but not much more than that. However, this fish meant food so Willy kept it and put it in the boat.

"The bite is on," Willy said aloud to himself as he remembered his dad saying that fish have particular times of the day that they like to eat. It seems these feeding times vary each day according to the settings of the moon and sun for that day. The fish will feed for a period of time and then suddenly stop. If you fish when

90

the bite is on you have a good chance of catching fish. He dropped the lure and sinker into the water again and began to row. A sudden jerk on the line jerked the boat and pulled it backward a bit.

"Wow!" exclaimed Willy. "This one must be a monster."

Willy rowed hard. Then as the line became extremely tight he stopped rowing briefly so that the line would slacken somewhat. Then as the line got slack Willy started rowing again. Over and over Willy worked the homemade oars for what seemed like hours to try to keep the fish tight on the line without letting it get so tight that it would break. Willy's arms and shoulders ached but he would not give up. Finally the action slowed down. A few minutes later, Willy had a big fish next to the boat. Seeing the boat, the fish dove for deeper water pulling the line out of Willy's hands. Once again Willy grabbed for the oars and rowed as hard as he could to tighten the line before the fish could throw the hook. Again he

91

worked the oars, almost like a professional by now, trying to keep the line tight so that he would not lose the fish.

Gradually the fish tired and when Willy realised that it was not pulling any more, he pulled the fish to the side of the boat. The fish moved its tail back and forth but was too tired to make a quick dive downwards. Willy quickly grabbed the fish quickly before it could get away. He could hardly lift it over the gunnel, the top edge of the boat's side, because it was so heavy. The fish tried to thrash its tail and Willy almost fell overboard into the water. As soon as he regained his balance, he reefed hard and the fish came flopping into the boat on top of him as he fell on his back onto the bottom of the boat. He must have looked silly but he was not hurt and he thought proudly, "If only Dad could see me now."

Willy pulled himself out from under the fish and sat up. He looked down and examined the fish he had just caught. It was very large but how heavy it was he was not sure. All of that hard work had made him even hungrier and thirstier than when he got up that morning. He knew he could not drink the salt water for drinking salt water tastes bad and only makes one thirstier. If you drink much of it, it can lead to mental instability. He decided to put away the fishing gear and head for shore. Before he had a chance to splash even one oar into the water, a faint rumbling sound wafted to him from along the shoreline.

"A car! It sounds like a car! Thanks God, for the car and the fish!" Willy declared excitedly. The oars moved fast and furiously as Willy headed for shore as quickly as possible.

When he beached the boat, Willy listened for the sound of the car that he thought he had heard but the sound was not there. Now he had to choose between two possibilities: He could go out on a search to find a road that might not even be there and hope to pick up a ride or he could cook a fish and then look for the road after he finished eating. Since the car, if there really had been a

93

car out there somewhere, could no longer be heard and the road, if there actually was a road, was not going to move anywhere anyway, Willy decided it was more important that he solve the problem of his growing hunger. A hungry boy's stomach comes first. Willy got out of the boat and headed toward the fire pit he had made earlier. Lunch was first on his agenda.

Willy gathered up some twigs scattered around the beach and soon had a fire started once more. He built up the fire with bigger and bigger pieces of wood. As his stone broiler was heating up, Willy went to the boat, took out the smaller fish killed it and with his filleting knife, cleaned the fish. He washed it in the salt water and then took it to the fire. He placed it on the stone roaster and waited for the salmon to cook.

CHAPTER EIGHT: A SPECIAL VISITOR

As Willy watched the cooking fish he thought of how bears like fish and hoped that none would show up on his beach. That would be one visitor that he would not want to meet. The thought made him shiver even though the weather was quite warm. He began to anxiously look around just to be certain no unwelcome visitor was around. A bit fearfully, Willy quietly prayed for God to protect him as he waited for the fish to cook.

The roasting salmon was almost cooked to perfection when Willy heard a distant voice to the north on the shore yelling to him. "Hello! Are you alright?"

Willy squinted his eyes and could see a Royal Canadian Mounted Police officer in his regular working uniform standing on the point of a small peninsula that jutted out at the other end of the bay on whose shore he was standing.

"No," Willy hollered. "I'm stranded!"

"Stay where you are. I'll come over to you," replied the police officer who walked up the peninsula into the woods and disappeared.

About a minute later Willy heard a car engine start in the trees somewhere above the point that the officer had been standing on. He followed the sound of the car's progress. Soon it was up on the ridge near the camping area above him. The sound of the car engine travelled to the area where Willy had camped the night before. Then the engine was turned off and he heard the sound of a car door closing. The police officer appeared at the edge of the ridge and then walked down to the fire to meet Willy.

"My name is Constable Dave White," said the policeman as he extended his right hand toward Willy. Willy liked his friendly attitude.

As Willy shook the officer's hand he replied, "I'm Willy, Willy MacNeil. The policeman looked astonished at this reply and stopped shaking Willy's hand.

96

"You're not Arthur MacNeil's son, are you?" Constable White asked.

"Yes," Willy replied beginning to feel concerned as to how a police officer that he did not know would know about his dad. "How do you know him?"

"Why don't we sit down and have some lunch and talk about it?" Constable White suggested. "It look's like you're quite a chef and you probably are quite hungry."

"Is he alright?" Willy blurted out, not wanting to eat until he knew about his dad.

Constable White replied with a smile, "Yes, he's alright and he'll be glad to know that you are too."

As they sat down on a couple of logs Willy gave the police officer some hot broiled salmon to eat along with him. Willy was eager to hear what the officer had to say, but instead suggested that they give thanks to God for the food first. The policeman agreed but rather embarrassingly suggested that Willy do the praying. Willy said, "Father, thank you for helping me catch this fish. Bless this food. And thank you so much for sending Constable White to find me, in Jesus' name, Amen."

Each of them began to eat their piece of the hot broiled fish and Willy blurted out, "What do you know about dad? Where is he?"

"Your dad is just fine. I never have met him but I know he is well at home. I'll tell you his story but first I have to report in to headquarters and tell them that you've been found," the officer told him. "You've given us all quite a scare. I also have to get a report from you as to what happened to you."

They walked up the ridge eating the fish as they went. The patrol car was parked by the old fire pit on top of the ridge but back far enough from the edge that they could not see it from the beach. The policeman opened the cruiser door and picked up the radio microphone. Willy could only make out part of the conversation but he heard enough to know that he was at a place called "King's Bay" on the mainland coast. Somehow the storm

98

had pushed Willy and the boat through the darkness of the channel and back to the mainland north of the island chain that they had gone through on Saturday morning. Willy was only twenty-eight kilometres (seventeen miles) or so from Eaglecrest, but he had not realised how close he was to home until now.

"Willy," Constable White said, "I just called off the search for you. The coast guard, search and rescue teams and private ships have been conducting a massive search for you around Big Island area since yesterday afternoon after the storm passed through. It is amazing that you drifted so far so fast without anyone seeing you. In fact, no-one even thought that it was possible for you to have drifted this far. I only came down this old logging trail because I had a strong feeling inside that I had to come here even though it is not a part of my regular patrol. I'm sure my supervisor won't mind now that I've found you. I'm sure glad I decided to take this road."

99

"Now, about your dad, Willy," he continued. "When the explosion took place, your dad jumped out of a cabin window into the sea. Your dad is a good swimmer and with a lifejacket on he had no trouble. He was afraid that you had been killed by the blast. The wind and waves obviously separated you quickly. Another fishing boat in the area heard the explosion and quickly came to rescue any survivors. They didn't see you but your dad climbed aboard the boat just as some sharks swam up. He got in just in time."

"Tell me about it!" replied Willy. "I know the feeling."

"Oh, you saw them too, did you?" Constable White asked.

"I sure did! They almost got me," Willy answered. Then he proceeded to tell the constable all about his adventures right up until the time that Constable White had arrived. The police officer wrote down the details in a

100

report book, stopping from time to time to ask questions about some of the details.

"Well, changing the subject, you've served me the main course but what about dessert?" Constable White asked jokingly.

"Right over here. No joke!" Willy replied laughing. He brought the R.C.M.P. officer down to the blackberry bushes. They each took a handful of berries.

"Well, I'll be! And fresh water too!" exclaimed the officer in unbelief. "You're lucky that this spring water is here. The pipe must have been put in years ago."

"God has been looking after me," Willy declared. Then Willy shared how that it was God who took care of him through all of his adventure, providing him with everything he needed.

"I used to say I was an atheist," the policeman told Willy, "but someone has surely been taking care of you. It is hard to believe that all of these events were just

101

coincidences. As I take you home you'll have to tell me more about your faith."

They pulled the boat up above the tide line and tied the bow to a big rock. Constable White looked in the boat and saw the fishing line and tackle still tied to the boat's seat. He looked over the homemade oars and oarlocks. Then he saw the big salmon in the boat. He shook his head in wonder. He took the big fish and helped Willy clean, wash and place it into a big garbage bag and then put it into the trunk of the patrol car. After this Willy and the constable got into the police car.

"I'll request a truck to come out and pick up your boat," Constable White remarked as he began to radio headquarters.

When the officer was done with the radio call Willy protested, "But sir, that's not my boat. It belongs to whoever lost it."

"I know, Willy, but we have to bring it in as an abandoned boat. We'll look for the owner when we get it back home. I just called it "your boat" because you were using it.

Constable White turned the ignition key, started the engine and they were off for home. The four by four trail turned on to an old dirt road winding through the heavy Pacific rain forest. After travelling for about nine or ten kilometers (six miles) the road became a gravel road with a few houses scattered along it on either side. About two kilometres (a little more than a mile) later, the gravel road turned on to the main highway to Eaglecrest.

Willy turned to Constable White and said in amazement, "I've been down this highway many times but never knew what was down this road."

"One thing I've discovered is that there is a lot yet to be discovered, even in our own back yard. Just when you think you know a great deal about something you discover how much you really do not know. We never stop learning, Willy. I guess that is the way it is with life." replied Constable White. "We always have more to learn.

103

Anyway, we'll soon be home and you can tell everyone all that you've been through and what you've learned."

CHAPTER NINE: A TIME FOR REJOICING

Mr. and Mrs. MacNeil, along with many friends, neighbours and reporters were waiting at the police station for the lost son to be returned. As they were headed for town, Constable White explained to Willy how that he had recently been transferred to the R.C.M.P. detachment in Eaglecrest. Since he was new to the area, he had not gotten to know many people in town. Now he knew Willy. Willy would be one of his first friends in Eaglecrest.

Constable White could not resist the temptation to add to the excitement of the return of this lost son. As he rounded the last corner to the police station, the officer flicked on the flashing blue and red lights and then sounded the siren to announce their arrival.

"Might as well come home to all these people in style," he told Willy. Willy just grinned with delight. He had always wanted to ride in a police cruiser and now he was doing so in style.

105

Willy had spent much of the time travelling home by sharing his own story of what Jesus could do in a person's life. He even got a promise that Constable White would join his family on the first Sunday that he was not working and go to church with them. He thought, "If nothing else happens but Constable White comes to Christ as I did, this will all be worth it."

When Willy got out of the police cruiser, he was swamped by people, hugging him, trying to shake his hands and asking all sorts of questions. Alongside his mom and dad were Pastor and Mrs. Benson and Mrs. Blaine, his Sunday School teacher. His dad embraced him and as Willy responded with a big hug of his own, his dad shouted, "Rejoice! My son which was lost is found! Welcome home, Wild Will!"

Willy stepped back a couple of steps and waited for the excitement to calm down. Looking at his friends and relatives his face was shining.

"Everybody," he boldly declared, "not only did this lost son come back his family and friends, but this lost son has come to God, his heavenly Father. I've asked Jesus to be my Saviour and to change me into a child of God. And has He ever done a number on me. It's wonderful! Pastor Benson, Mrs. Blaine, Mom and Dad, please forgive me for doubting your words about God. I was so wrong, but now I understand. The lost really is found!'

There was tremendous happiness at this announcement. His mom and dad both hugged him and his dad said, "I'm so happy, son. You'll have to tell us all about it when all of this excitement is over." People were crying for joy and praising God. Some were trying to shake Willy's hand again. A few reporters stood by not quite sure what to make of it all but grinning along with the rest of the people. In the unseen heavenly realm angels were rejoicing too. Jesus said that there is much joy and celebrating in heaven over one soul that repents.

When things calmed down a bit, Constable White moved to the back of the patrol car. He opened the trunk of the cruiser. "You've got to get this smelly thing out of my trunk," he joked to Willy.

Willy went to the trunk and Constable White helped him lift out the garbage bag. When he pulled out the fish someone ran to get a scale to weigh it. It weighed in at just over twenty-two pounds on the scale. It was not quite heavy enough to be classed as a "tyee" which must be over thirty pounds to rate as one of these trophy salmon but it created a lot of excitement. Besides it had been cleaned and then weighed. No-one would ever actually know what the full weight of the salmon really was. Reporters shouted, flash cameras went off and excitement reigned again until finally everyone, happy and a bit weary, headed for home. There was an exciting story for the reporters to print in the Eaglecrest Chronicle for Monday morning. It had been quite a day for everyone.

The next Sunday the whole MacNeil family went to church. This time all of them were happy to go and were ready to worship God from a grateful heart. Also, this time a stranger joined them. Constable White had this Sunday off work and he joined them for the church service as he had promised Willy.

After the church service was over, Constable White went with the MacNeils to their home for lunch. On the way there he said, "I'm beginning to think that there really is something to this Christianity thing. I have seen and heard so much that I have never come across before. You Christians are different. In a good sense, I mean. There were some things at the church that I didn't really understand though."

Mr. MacNeil offered, "Any time you're ready, we can talk about it."

"Thanks. I'd like that, Arthur," Dave White replied.

Part way home, Constable White had them make a detour by way of the police station. On the way, Willy

109

asked his dad, "What are you going to do about a fishing boat now?"

"No problem, son. The insurance company is investigating the accident and have promised that when they are done they will pay me enough insurance money for a new one. They have already determined that the disaster was accidental. I will start looking for a new boat right away; a diesel-powered one this time. The new one will have GPS (Global Positioning System). It will have all of the modern navigational tools to make sailing easier. Granted, my insurance premiums will probably go up, but I guess that means that I'll have to take you with me to the saltchuck so that we can catch more fish to pay for the increase in cost," Mr. MacNeil said with his customary grin. "You've already proven that you can catch fish." Willy was delighted with that.

The family car stopped at the police station. Constable White took the family around to the locked yard at the back of the station. He unlocked the gate and opened it. They walked over to where some stolen and lost items that people had found were kept. "There's your boat," the officer told Willy.

There was the old boat cleaned up and painted white and blue with a red pin stripe down the sides. Two new oars were fitted into shiny oarlocks. The old oars, oarlock posts and first aid box were lying in the bottom as souvenirs of Willy's adventure.

"I,I,I don't understand," stammered Willy. "I thought that you were looking for the rightful owner."

"Well," replied Constable White, "we did a thorough check and discovered that though this boat has never been registered, it belonged to an old man who lived on the coast just north of here. He died about a month ago and had no relatives or heirs left for what little he left behind. I guess we have to call it salvage, so, since you retrieved it, the boat is yours. The fellows at the precinct couldn't imagine giving a beat-up old boat to the one who put our little town on the map by getting lost, especially after taking it away from him. Everyone chipped in and fixed it up for you. You can pick it up this week. Okay?"

"Okay?" said Willy as tears of joy coursed down his cheeks. "Okay?" he repeated as he gave Constable White a big hug. "It's not only okay. It's awesome, it's rad, it's wonderful! Thank you so much!"

Right then Willy decided to get the biggest Thank-you card he could find and bring it to the station for all of the wonderful people at the police station who made this possible for him.

Constable White gave a secret wink to Mr. MacNeil and then put on his face the sternest look that he could produce. Scowling down at Willy he said, "Young fellow, if you are going to keep this boat you will have to assure me that there'll be no more of this getting lost business."

112

Willy looked up at him and solemnly declared, "This is one lost son that has been found and I plan to keep it that way."

Everyone else began to laugh and Willy, realising it was all a joke, joined them in their laughter as they turned to go home. He knew that God works out all things for our good if we love God and serve Him as His children. Somehow Willy also just knew that being found was the beginning of many good things to come.

Join me on my next adventure soon.

70591164R00064

Made in the USA
Columbia, SC
13 May 2017